The Conc

A Po

Second edition

The Concise PRINCE2®

A Pocket Guide

Second edition

COLIN BENTLEY

IT Governance Publishing

Every possible effort has been made to ensure that the information contained in this book is accurate at the time of going to press, and the publisher and the author cannot accept responsibility for any errors or omissions, however caused. Any opinions expressed in this book are those of the author, not the publisher. Websites identified are for reference only, not endorsement, and any website visits are at the reader's own risk. No responsibility for loss or damage occasioned to any person acting, or refraining from action, as a result of the material in this publication can be accepted by the publisher or the author.

PRINCE2® is a registered trade mark of the Cabinet Office.

Apart from any fair dealing for the purposes of research or private study, or criticism or review, as permitted under the Copyright, Designs and Patents Act 1988, this publication may only be reproduced, stored or transmitted, in any form, or by any means, with the prior permission in writing of the publisher or, in the case of reprographic reproduction, in accordance with the terms of licences issued by the Copyright Licensing Agency. Enquiries concerning reproduction outside those terms should be sent to the publisher at the following address:

IT Governance Publishing
IT Governance Limited
Unit 3, Clive Court, Bartholomew's Walk
Cambridgeshire Business Park
Ely, Cambridgeshire
CB7 4EA
United Kingdom

www.itgovernance.co.uk

© Colin Bentley 2012, 2013

The author has asserted the rights of the author under the Copyright, Designs and Patents Act, 1988, to be identified as the author of this work.

First published in the United Kingdom in 2012 by
IT Governance Publishing.

Second edition published in 2013.

ISBN 978-1-84928-478-3

FOREWORD

Many books have been written about PRINCE2. The only problem is that where they try to cover all of the method, they are BIG books that take a lot of reading.

This book is intended as a refresher; a reminder of all the salient points of the method without drowning you in detail. You don't need to skip, don't need to 'cherry-pick'. In one brief document, it reminds you of the essentials of the method. It is an ideal basis for anyone, for example, who is preparing for the PRINCE2 Foundation exam or setting out on their first few PRINCE2 projects. In a flash you can remind yourself of any part of the method, using it as a checklist that you are on the right road to a successful project.

The book fits easily into a pocket or handbag and is an ideal refresher or learning aid as you travel to work, for example, on the train or on a plane. Its easy-to-read, rubric style lends itself to quick absorption of the keys to the method.

ABOUT THE AUTHOR

Colin Bentley has been a project manager since 1966 and has managed many projects, large and small, in several countries. He has been working with PRINCE2, PRINCE and its predecessor, PROMPT II, since 1975. He was one of the team that brought PROMPT II to the marketplace, wrote the major part of the PRINCE2 manual and is the author of all revisions to the manual until the 2009 version.

He was the Chief Examiner for PRINCE2 from its beginning until 2008 and wrote all Foundation and Practitioner exam papers, and marked them until they reached the massive volumes that are sat today.

Now retired, he has had over twenty books published, has lectured widely on PRINCE2 and has acted as project management consultant to such firms as The London Stock Exchange, Microsoft Europe, Tesco Stores, Commercial Union and the BBC. He still writes books on the PRINCE2 method and has updated them all to reflect the 2009 version.

ACKNOWLEDGEMENTS

The book acknowledges the information contained in the PRINCE2 manual, 2009 edition. PRINCE2® is a registered trade mark of the Cabinet Office.

CONTENTS

Introduction 1
   Overview 1
   Principles: 2
Chapter 1: Processes 3
   Starting up a project 3
   Directing a project 3
   Initiating a project 3
   Controlling a stage 12
   Managing product delivery 12
   Managing a stage boundary 12
   Closing a project 12
Chapter 2: Themes 29
   Business Case 29
   Organisation 31
   Plans 35
   Quality 37
   Risks 40
   Change 42
   Progress 44
Chapter 3: Techniques 51
   Product-based planning 51
   Quality review 52
Chapter 4: Tailoring 55
   Existing terms, procedures and forms 55
   Business Case 55
   Organisation 55
   Documentation 56
   Plans 57
   Quality 57
   Risk 57
   Change 57
   Progress 58
Glossary of Terms 59
ITG Resources 61

INTRODUCTION

Overview

What is a project?

A project is a temporary organisation for the purpose of delivering one or more business products according to an agreed Business Case.

What makes projects different?

- temporary
- cross-functional team
- more risky than BAU (Business As Usual)
- bring about change
- unique.

Project variables to be controlled:

- costs
- timescales
- quality
- scope
- risk
- benefits.

PRINCE2 benefits:

- can be applied to any type of project
- projects are driven by viability of a Business Case
- recognition of responsibilities
- product focus
- different plan levels for different management levels
- tolerance setting / management by exception
- stakeholder involvement throughout the project life
- all projects share common vocabulary
- promotes consistency of project work

Introduction

- established and proven method
- supports project management learning and continuous improvement
- provides assurance, assessment and audit capabilities
- wide expertise support
- exam-based accreditation.

Principles:

- continued business justification
- learn from experience
- defined roles and responsibilities
- manage by stages
- manage by exception
- focus on products
- tailor to suit the project environment.

CHAPTER 1: PROCESSES

Starting up a project

Purpose

- To answer the question, 'Do we have a viable and worthwhile project?'
- To ensure prerequisites for DP (directing a project) and authorisation of IP (initiating a project) are in place.

(*See Table 1: Starting up a project*.)

Directing a project

Purpose

- To enable the Project Board to be accountable for the project's success by making key decisions and exercising overall control.

(*See Table 2: Directing a project*.)

Initiating a project

Purpose

- To establish solid foundations for the project.
- To enable the Project Board to understand everything about the project – the cost, time, benefits and risks – before committing to major expenditure.

(*See Table 3: Initiating a project*.)

Table 1: Starting up a project

Activity	Input	From	By	Output
Appoint the Executive and Project Manager	Project mandate	Corporate or programme management	Corporate or programme management	Executive and Project Manager role descriptions
			Project Manager (PM)	Daily Log
Prepare the outline Business Case	Project mandate	Corporate or programme management	Executive	Outline Business Case
Capture previous lessons	Previous lesson reports	Quality assurance	Project Manager	Lessons Log
Design and appoint the project management team	Executive appointment	Corporate or programme management	PM - produce Exec - approve	Project management team structure and role descriptions
Select the project approach and assemble the Project Brief	Project mandate	Corporate or programme management	Project Manager	Project approach Project Brief
Plan the initiation stage	Project Brief		Project Manager	Initiation Stage Plan
			Project Manager	*Request to initiate a project*

Table 2: Directing a project

Activity	Input	From	By	Output
Authorise initiation	*Request to initiate a project*	Project Manager (SU)	Project Board	*Initiation notification*
	Project Brief	Project Manager (SU)		
	Project Product Description	Project Manager (SU)		
	Project management team appointments	Project Manager (SU)		
	Initiation Stage Plan	Project Manager (SU)	Project Board	*Authority to initiate a project*
Authorise the project	*Request to deliver a project*	Project Manager (IP)	Project Board	*Stage authorisation*
	Project Initiation Documentation (PID)	Project Manager (IP)	Project Board	*Project authorisation notification*
	Benefits Review Plan	Project Manager (IP)		

1: Processes

Activity	Input	From	By	Output
Give ad hoc direction	Request for advice	Project Manager (CS)	Project Board	*Advice and decisions*
	Highlight Reports	Project Manager (CS)		
	Exception Report	Project Manager (CS)	Project Board	*Exception Plan request/Premature close*
	Advice and decisions	Corporate or programme management	Project Board	*Premature close or new issue*
Authorise a Stage or Exception Plan	Request to approve Stage / Exception Plan	Project Manager (SB)	Project Board	*Stage or Exception Plan approval*
	End Stage Report	Project Manager (SB)		
	Next Stage Plan or Exception Plan	Project Manager (SB)		
	New Product Descriptions	Project Manager (SB)		
	Project Plan	Project Initiation Documentation		

1: Processes

Authorise a Stage or Exception Plan cont.	Business Case	Project Initiation Documentation	
	Lessons Report (optional)	Project Manager (SB)	
Authorise project closure	End Project Report	Project Manager (CP)	Project Board
	Closure recommendation	Project Manager (CP)	*Closure notification*
	Original PID		
	Lessons Report	Project Manager (CP)	Project Board *Lessons Report*
	Follow-on action recommendations	Project Manager (CP)	Project Board *Follow-on action recommendations*
	Benefits Review Plan	Executive	Project Board *Benefits Review Plan (to corporate)*

Table 3: Initiating a project

Activity	Input	From	By	Output
Prepare the Risk Management Strategy	*Authority to initiate the project*	Project Board (DP)	Project Manager	Risk Management Strategy
	Project Brief	Project Manager (SU)	Project Support	Risk Register
	Daily Log	Project Manager (SU)		
	Lessons Log	Project Manager (SU)		
Prepare the Configuration Management Strategy	Project Brief, Daily Log, Lessons Log and Risk Register		Project Manager	Configuration Management Strategy
			Project Support	Configuration Item Records
			Project Support	Issue Register
			Project Manager	Updated PMT team structure
			Project Manager	Updated role descriptions

Prepare the Quality Management Strategy	Project Product Description	Project Manager (SU)	Project Manager	Quality Management Strategy
	Project Brief, Lessons Log, Risk Register and Issue Register		Project Support	Quality Register
Prepare the Communication Management Strategy	Project Brief, Lessons Log, Risk, Quality and Configuration Management Strategy		Project Manager	Communication Management Strategy
	Risk Register	Project Support		
	Issue Register	Project Support		
Set up the project controls	Project Plan	Project Manager (IP)	Project Manager	Project controls (part of PID)

1: Processes

Activity	Input	From	By	Output
Set up the project controls cont.	Lessons Log, Project Brief, Quality, Configuration, Risk and Communication Management Strategies		Project Manager	Updated project management team structure
			Project Manager	Updated role Descriptions
Create the Project Plan	Lessons Log, Risk Register, Issue Register, Project Brief, Project Product Description, Quality, Configuration, Risk and Communication Management Strategies		Project Manager	Project Plan

1: Processes

			Project Plan
			Updated PMT structure
			Updated role descriptions
Refine the Business Case	Outline Business Case	Executive (SU)	Detailed Business Case
	Project Plan	Project Manager (IP)	Benefits Review Plan
	Risk Register	Project Support	
Assemble the Project Initiation Documentation	(Detailed) Business Case, Project Plan, Quality, Risk and Communication Management Strategies		Project Initiation Documentation
			Request to deliver a project
			Stage boundary approaching

1: Processes

Controlling a stage

Purpose

- To assign and monitor work, deal with issues and risks, report progress and take action to ensure that the stage stays within its tolerances.

(*See Table 4: Controlling a stage.*)

Managing product delivery

Purpose

- To act as a link between the Team Manager and the Project Manager.
- To cover the requirements for accepting, executing and delivering project work.

(*See Table 5: Managing product delivery.*)

Managing a stage boundary

Purpose

- To provide the Project Board with enough information to confirm continued viability and acceptability of risks.

(*See Table 6: Managing a stage boundary.*)

Closing a project

Purpose

- To obtain confirmation that the project product has been accepted.
- To recognise that the objectives in the Project Initiation Documentation (PID) and agreed changes have been achieved (i.e. recognise that the project has nothing more to contribute).

1: Processes

(*See Table 7: Closing a project.*)

Table 4: Controlling a stage

Activity	Input	From	By	Output
Authorise a Work Package	Stage authorisation	Project Board (DP)	Project Manager	Work Package
	Stage Plan	Project Manager (SB)	Project Support	Updated Configuration Item Records
	Product Descriptions	Project Manager (SB)	Project Support	Updated Quality Register
	Team Plan(s)	Team Manager (MP)	Project Manager	Updated Risk Register
	PID	Project Manager (IP)	Project Manager	Updated Issue Register
	(Corrective action)	Project Manager (CS)		
Review Work Package status	Stage Plan		Project Manager	Updated Stage Plan
	Work Package	Team Manager	Project Support	Updated Configuration Item Records
	Checkpoint Report	Team Manager	Project Manager	Updated Risk Register
	Quality Register	Project Support	Project Manager	Updated Issue Register
	Team Plan(s)	Team Manager(s)	Project Manager	Updated Work Package
	Risk Register	Project Manager		

1: Processes

Receive completed Work Packages	Stage Plan		Project Manager	Updated Stage Plan
	Configuration Item Records	Project Support	Project Support	Updated Configuration Item Records
	Quality Register	Project Support		
Review the stage status	Stage Plan	Project Manager	Project Manager	Updated Stage Plan
	Quality Register	Project Support	Project Manager	Updated Lessons Log
Review the stage status cont.	Product Status Account	Project Support		
	Checkpoint Report(s)	Team Manager	Project Manager	Issue Report (optional)
	Issue Register	Project Manager	Project Manager	Updated Issue Register
	Risk Register	Project Manager	Project Manager	Updated Risk Register
	Business Case	PID		
	Project Plan	PID		
	Benefits Review Plan	PID		

1: Processes

Activity	Input	From	By	Output
Report highlights	Stage Plan	Team Manager(s)	Project Manager	Highlight Report
	Checkpoint Reports			
	Daily Log	Project Manager		
	Lessons Log	Project Manager		
	Quality Register	Project Support		
	Risk Register	Project Manager		
	Issue Register	Project Manager		
	Product Status Account	Project Support		
	Previous Highlight Reports			
	Communication Management Strategy	PID		
Capture and examine issues and risks	New issues		Project Manager	Updated Issue Register
	New risks		Project Manager	Issue Report

Capture and examine issues and risks cont.	Stage Plan		Project Manager	Updated Risk Register
	Business Case	PID	Project Manager	Request for advice
	Project Plan	PID		
	Communication Management Strategy	PID		
	Configuration Management Strategy	PID		
Escalate issues and risks	Issue Report		Project Manager	Exception Report
	Issue Register	Project Manager	Project Manager	Updated Issue Register
	Risk Register	Project Manager	Project Manager	Updated Risk Register

1: Processes

Activity	Input	From	By	Output
Escalate issues and risks cont.	Business Case	PID	Project Manager	Updated Issue Report
Take corrective action	Daily Log	Project Manager	Project Manager	Updated Daily Log
	Issue Register	Project Manager	Project Manager	Updated Issue Register
	Risk Register	Project Manager	Project Manager	Updated Risk Register
	Issue Report		Project Manager	Updated Issue Report
	Stage Plan		Project Manager	Updated Stage Plan
	Configuration Item Records	Project Support	Project Support	Updated Configuration Item Records

1: Processes

Table 5: Managing product delivery

Activity	Input	From	By	Output
Accept a Work Package	Work Package	Project Manager (CS)	Team Manager	Team Plan
			Project Support	Updated Quality Register
			Team Manager	New risk (optional)
Execute a Work Package	Work Package	Project Manager (CS)	Team Manager	*Specialist products*
	Team Plan	Team Manager	Project Support	Updated Quality Register
			Project Support	Updated Configuration Item Record
			Team Manager	Updated Team Plan
			Team Manager	Checkpoint Report(s)
			Team Manager	Approval records
			Team Manager	New risk
			Team Manager	New issue

1: Processes

Activity	Input	From	By	Output
Deliver a Work Package	Work Package	Project Manager (CS)	Team Manager	Updated/ Completed Work Package
	Quality Register	Project Support	Team Manager	Updated Team Plan
	Configuration Item Records	Project Support		

Table 6: Managing a stage boundary

Activity	Input	From	By	Output
Plan the next stage	*Stage boundary approaching*	Project Manager (CS)	Project Manager	
	Current Stage Plan	Project Manager (CS)	Project Manager	Next Stage Plan
	Project Plan	PID	Project Manager	Updated Project Plan
	Issue Register	Project Manager	Project Manager	Updated Issue Register
	Risk Register	Project Manager	Project Manager	Updated Risk Register
	Project Product Description	PID	Project Support	Configuration Item Record(s)
	Project approach	PID	Project Manager	Any revisions to project approach
	Strategies	PID	Project Manager	Any new Product Description(s)
			Project Support	Updated Quality Register
	Project management team	PID	Project Manager	Updated PMT

1: Processes

Activity	Input	From	By	Output
Produce an Exception Plan	*Exception Plan request*	Project Board		
	Exception Report	Project Manager (CS)		
	Current Stage Plan	Project Manager (CS)	Project Manager	Exception Plan
	Project Plan	PID	Project Manager	Updated Project Plan
	Issue Register	Project Manager	Project Manager	Updated Issue Register
	Risk Register	Project Manager	Project Manager	Updated Risk Register
	Project Product Description	PID	Project Support	Configuration Item Record(s)
	Project approach	PID	Project Manager	Any revisions to project approach
	Quality Management Strategy	PID	Project Manager	Any new Product Description(s)
			Project Support	Updated Quality Register

1: Processes

Update the Project Plan	Project Plan	PID	Project Manager	Updated Project Plan
	Current Stage Plan	Project Manager (CS)		
	Next Stage Plan	Project Manager (SB)		
	Project approach	PID	Project Manager	Any revisions to project approach
	Issue Register		Project Manager	Updated Issue Register
	Risk Register		Project Manager	Updated Risk Register
Update the Business Case	Business Case	PID	Project Manager	Updated Business Case
	Benefits Review Plan	PID	Project Manager	Updated Benefits Review Plan
	Project Plan	PID		
	Issue Register		Project Manager	Updated Issue Register
	Risk appetite (any revision)	Corporate / programme management		
	Risk Register		Project Manager	Updated Risk Register

1: Processes

Activity	Input	From	By	Output
Report stage end	Project Plan	PID	Project Manager	End Stage Report
	Current Stage Plan			

Table 7: Closing a project

Activity	Input	From	By	Output
Prepare planned closure	*Project end approaching*	Project Manager (CS)		
	Product Status Account	Project Support		
	Project Plan	PID	Project Manager	Updated Project Plan
	Current Stage Plan	Project Manager (CS)		
	Project Product Description	PID		
Prepare premature closure	*Premature close instruction*			
	Product Status Account	Project Support		
	Project Plan	PID	Project Manager	Updated Project Plan
	Current Stage Plan	Project Manager (CS)	Project Manager	*Additional work estimates*
	Project Product Description	PID		

1: Processes

Activity	Input	From	By	Output
	Issue Register	Project Manager	Project Manager	Updated Issue Register
	Issue Report (optional)	Project Manager (CS)	Project Manager	Updated Issue Report (optional)
Hand over products	Acceptance records	Users (Project Manager to obtain)	Project Manager	Follow-on action recommendations
	Issue Register	Project Manager	Project Support	Updated Configuration Item Record
	Risk Register	Project Manager	Project Manager	Benefits Review Plan
	Configuration Management Strategy	PID		
	Acceptance	Operations and maintenance groups		
Evaluate the project	PID		Project Manager	End Project Report
	Follow-on action recommendations		Project Manager	Lessons Report

1: Processes

Recommend project closure	Communication Management Strategy	PID	Project Manager	Closure recommendation
			Project Manager	Closed Issue Register
			Project Manager	Closed Risk Register
			Project Manager	Closed Quality Register
			Project Manager	Closed Lessons Log
			Project Manager	Closed Daily Log
	Configuration Management Strategy	PID	Project Support	Archived project records

27

CHAPTER 2: THEMES

Business Case

Purpose

- To set up mechanisms to judge whether the project is (and remains) viable, desirable *and achievable* in order to support decisions on its (continued) investment.

Summary

- No project should start without business justification.
- If the justification disappears, the project should be stopped.
- The Business Case drives decision-making.
- Benefits should be measurable.
- Most benefits are realised post-project.
- Risk and change evaluation should include impact on Business Case.

Table 8: Business Case lifecycle

Develop	SU & IP
Maintain	SB
Verify	DP
Confirm	Post-project and DP (any mid-project benefits)

Table 9: Basic business options

Do nothing	Do the minimum	Do something

2: Themes

Related principles

- Continued business justification.

Answers

- Why?
- Can the project (still) be justified?

Who

Table 10: Responsibilities – Business Case

Product	Responsible	When
Outline Business Case	Executive	SU
Expected benefits	Senior User	IP
Detailed Business Case	Executive	IP
Impact of changes or risks	Project Manager	CS
Impact from Project Plan changes or revised benefit figures	Project Manager	SB
Any benefits already? Benefits Review Plan	Project Manager Executive	CP
Benefit realisation	Senior User	Post-project

Special terms

Table 11: Special terms

Output	Any tangible or intangible specialist product created by the project
Outcome	Result of the change derived from using the project's products
Benefit	An advantage, help or aid provided by one or more end products of the project as perceived by one or more users
Dis-benefit	Actual consequences of an activity, perceived to have a negative impact by one or more stakeholders

Organisation

Purpose

- To define the lines of authority and WHO is responsible for what.

Summary

- PRINCE2 believes that every project has a CUSTOMER who will specify and use the end product and a SUPPLIER who will provide the resources to build that product.
- A successful project relies on controlled leadership, which requires good communications.
- Every project needs (decision-making) representation from business, user and supplier.
- There are four management levels.

2: Themes

Table 12: Four management levels

Corporate or programme management
Project Board
Project Manager
Team Manager

- Roles can be shared or combined.
- Project Board = decision-making + accountability.

2: Themes

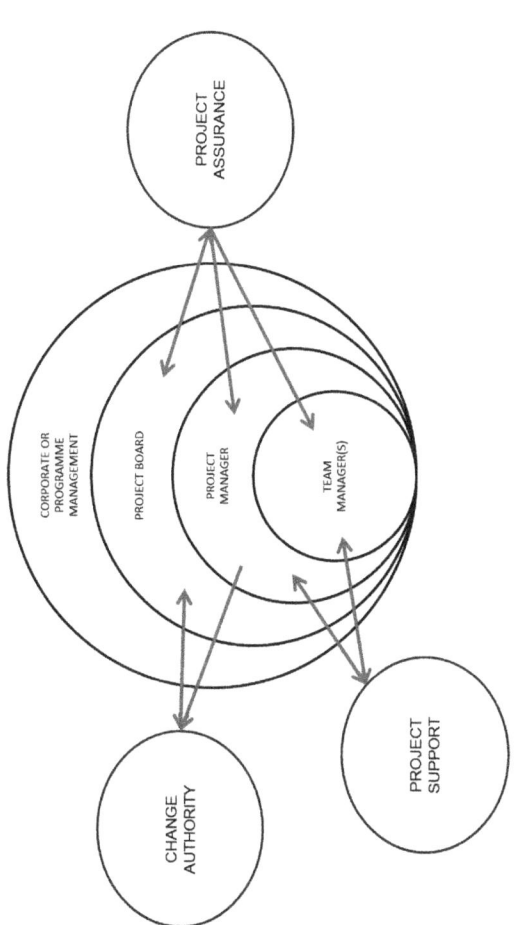

Figure 1: Project management team

2: Themes

- Project Board members can delegate some activities (not decisions) to Project Assurance.
- Project Board may appoint a Change Authority to handle change requests.
- Project management team (PMT) should be reviewed at every stage end (SB) to see if changes are needed.
- Stakeholders = non-decision-makers, but need to be kept informed.
- Communication needs of stakeholders defined in Communication Management Strategy.
- Communication needs of Project Board defined in project controls.

Related principles

Defined roles and responsibilities.

Answers

- Accountability.
- Who is responsible for what?
- Who reports to whom?

Who

Table 13: Responsibilities – organisation

Product	Responsible	When
Executive appointment	Corporate / programme	SU
Project Manager appointment	Executive	SU
Project management team design	Project Manager	SU
Project management team changes	Project Manager + Project Board	SB

2: Themes

Special terms

- Executive
- Senior User
- Senior Supplier
- Project Board
- Project Assurance
- Project Support
- Project Manager
- Team Manager
- Change Authority

Plans

Purpose

- To define the what, how, where, when and by whom products are to be created.

Summary

- Provides a baseline for measuring progress.
- Enables thinking ahead.
- Helps avoid omissions and duplication.
- Helps identify threats and opportunities.
- Facilitates communication and control.
- Provides a basis for control.

2: Themes

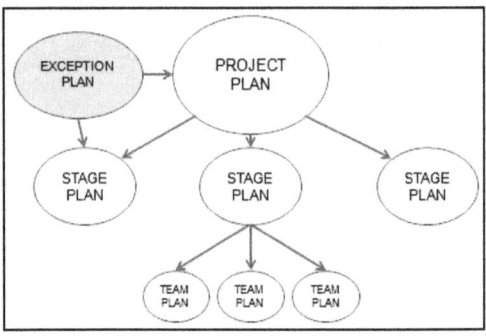

Figure 2: Levels of plan

Planning steps

- Design the plan.
- Define and analyse the products - using product-based planning (PBP) technique.
- Identify activities and dependencies.
- Prepare estimates.
- Prepare the schedule.
- Document the plan.

And in each step ANALYSE THE RISKS.

Related principles

- Focus on products
- Manage by stages.

Answers

- What?
- How?
- When?
- Who?
- Are the targets achievable?

2: Themes

Who

Table 14: Responsibilities – plans

Product	Responsible	When
Initiation Stage Plan	Project Manager	SU
Project Plan	Project Manager	IP
Stage Plans	Project Manager	SB
Team Plans	Team Manager	MP

Special terms

- Product breakdown structure
- Product flow diagram
- Product Description
- Exception Plan

Quality

Purpose

- To define and implement how the project will create and verify products that are fit for purpose.

Summary

- ISO9000 definition of quality: 'Totality of features and inherent or assigned characteristics of a product that bear on its ability to show that it meets its requirements.'
- Aim of theme: common understanding of the criteria against which the quality of the project's products will be assessed.
- Quality of management as well as specialist products.

2: Themes

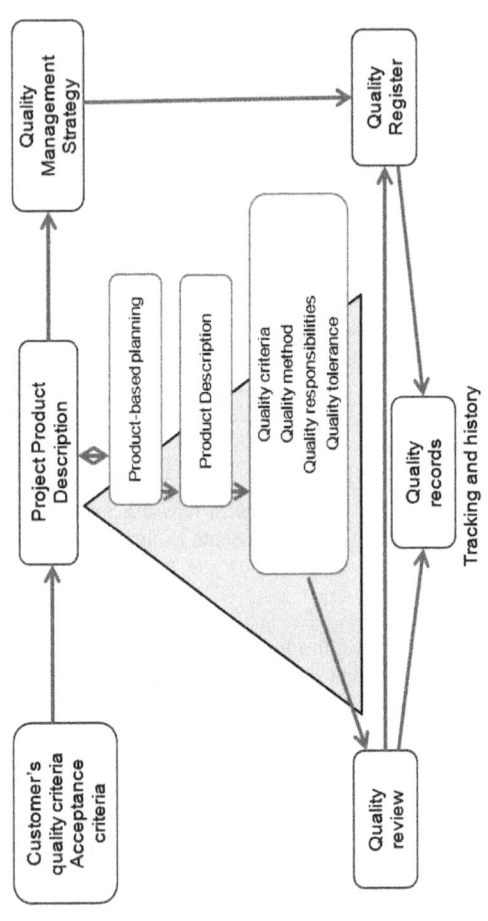

Figure 3: PRINCE2 approach to quality

Table 15: Quality acceptance criteria

	Acceptance criteria
MoSCoW	**M**ust have
	Should have
	Could have
	Won't have for now

Table 16: Quality review

Quality review	Input	Output
Preparation	Product Product Description Invitation	Question lists Annotated copies
Review	Product	Follow-up action list Updated Quality Register Updated Configuration Item Record (CIR)
Follow-up	Follow-up action list	Sign-off Updated Quality Register Updated Configuration Item Record
Roles	Chair Presenter Reviewer Administrator	

Related principles

- Focus on products
- Learn from experience.

Answers

- Will products meet business expectations?

- Will the desired benefits be achieved subsequently?

Who

Table 17: Responsibilities – quality

Product	Responsible	When
Customer's quality expectations	Senior User	SU
Project Product Description	Project Manager	SU
Quality Management Strategy	Project Manager	IP
Quality Register	Project Support	IP
Product Descriptions	Project Manager	IP (Project Plan), SB

Special terms

- Customer's quality expectations (CQE)
- Product Description
- Quality criteria
- Quality review
- Quality assurance – site-wide – independent of project

Risks

Purpose

- To identify, assess and control uncertainty.

Summary

- Risk is an uncertain event or set of events that, should it occur, will have an effect on the achievement of objectives.
- Threat – negative effect.
- Opportunity – positive effect.

Table 18: Risk management procedure

Risk management procedure			
1 Identify	2 Assess	3 Plan	4 Implement
5 Communicate			

Identify – cause / event / effect

Table 19: Risk responses

Threat	Opportunity
Avoid	Exploit
Reduce	Enhance
Fallback	Reject
Transfer	
Accept	
Share	Share

Related principles

- Continued business justification.

Answers

- Probability – how likely
- Impact – how much
- Proximity – how soon

2: Themes

Who

Table 20: Responsibilities – risk

Product	Responsible	When
Risk appetite	Corporate / Programme	SU
Risk Management Strategy	Project Manager	IP
Risk Register	Project Support	IP

Special terms

Table 21: Special terms

Risk appetite	Amount of risk an organisation considers acceptable
Risk tolerance	Risk threshold that, when threatened, will trigger an Exception Report
Risk owner	Responsible for the management, monitoring and control of an assigned risk
Risk actionee	Assigned to carry out a risk response action
Risk profile	Probability / Impact grid showing risk tolerances boundary
Risk budget	Sum of money set aside for fallback plans *and* for responses to risks not identified during IP

Change

Purpose

- To identify, assess, control potential and approved changes to the baseline.

Summary

- Covers issue and change control and configuration management.

Table 22: Issue and change control procedure

Issue and change control procedure				
Capture	Examine	Propose	Decide	Implement

Table 23: Types of issue

Request for change (RFC)	Off-specification (O-S)	Problem / Concern

Related principles

- Continued business justification
- Manage by exception
- Defined roles and responsibilities

Answers

- What does anyone want to change, delete or add after the Project Initiation Documentation has been agreed?
- What would be the impact of a change?
- Product status.

Who

Table 24: Responsibilities – change

Product	Responsible	When
Configuration Management Strategy	Project Manager	IP
Configuration Item Record(s)	Project Manager	SB
Daily Log	Project Manager	SU
Issue Register	Project Support	IP
Issue Report	Project Manager	CS
Product Status Account	Project Support	CS/SB

Special terms

Table 25: Special terms

Change Authority	Project Board delegates some decisions on changes within limits
Change budget	Funds changes and analysis costs; linked to Change Authority
Concession	Acceptance by the Project Board of a product that fails to fully meet its specification

Progress

Purpose

To establish mechanisms to:
- compare actual progress against planned
- forecast project completion
- review continued viability
- control unacceptable deviations.

2: Themes

Summary

Progress controls ensure that, for each level of the project management team, the next higher level can:

- monitor progress
- compare level of achievement with plan
- review plans and options against future situations
- detect problems and identify risks
- authorise future work.

Table 26: Progress controls

IN	OUT
\multicolumn{2}{Corporate / programme management}
Overall requirements Project tolerances	Project progress / exceptions
\multicolumn{2}{Project Board}
Stage authorisations Stage tolerances	PID New Stage Plans Highlight Reports End Stage Reports Exception Reports End Project Report
IN	OUT
\multicolumn{2}{Project Manager}
Work Package + tolerances	Checkpoint Reports
\multicolumn{2}{Team Manager}

Tolerances define the amount of discretion that each management level can exercise without the need to refer up to the next level for approval. (*See Table 27.*)

Table 27: Tolerances

Area	Project level	Stage level	Work Package level	Product
Time	Project Plan	Stage Plan	Work Package	
Cost	Project Plan	Stage Plan	Work Package	
Scope	Project Plan	Stage Plan	Work Package	
Risk	Risk Management Strategy	Stage Plan	Work Package	
Quality	Project Product Description			Product Description
Benefits	Business Case			

2: Themes

An exception is a situation where it can be forecast that there will be a deviation beyond the agreed tolerance levels.

Management stages

- Partitions of the project with management decision points.
- Collection of activities and products whose delivery is managed as a unit.
- The element of work delegated by the Project Board to the Project Manager at any one time.

Table 28: Management stage benefits

Management stage benefits
Gives the Project Board the opportunity to assess project viability at key moments
Allows key decisions to be made prior to the detailed work needed to implement them
Facilitates management by exception by authorising only one stage at a time
Business Case and Project Plan are reviewed before committing to a stage
Project Manager can make adjustments as long as within stage tolerances

Number of stages criteria:

- Must be at least two (initiation and the rest of the project).
- How far ahead is it sensible to plan?
- When are the key decision points?
- How risky is the project? (More risks = shorter stages.)
- Too many short stages increase management overhead.
- Too few, long stages reduce Project Board control.
- Project Board and Project Manager confidence levels.

2: Themes

Event-driven controls:

- End Stage Reports
- End Project Report
- Exception Report
- Project Initiation Documentation completion

Time-driven controls:

- Checkpoint Reports
- Highlight Reports

Technical stages

- Product Description(s) should specify relationship between management and technical stages.
- Often overlap – management stages do not.
- Covers stages such as design, build and implementation.

Related principles

- Manage by exception.
- Continued business justification.
- Manage by stages.

Answers

- Where are we now?
- How does this compare with where we planned to be?
- Is the project still viable?
- Are we still confident in the way forward?

Who

Table 29: Responsibilities – progress

Product	Responsible	When
Checkpoint Report	Team Manager	Frequency agreed in Work Package
Highlight Report	Project Manager	Frequency agreed with Project Board
End Stage Report	Project Manager	End of stage
Exception Report	Project Manager	Forecast tolerance exception
End Project Report	Project Manager	Close of project

Special terms

Table 30: Special terms

Tolerance	Permissible deviation above and below a planned target
Exception	A forecast deviation beyond the agreed tolerance

CHAPTER 3: TECHNIQUES

Product-based planning

PRINCE2 planning philosophy is to first identify the required products, then the activities, dependencies and resources required to deliver the products. There are four tasks in product-based planning.

Table 31: Product-based planning tasks

TASK	WHEN	DESCRIPTION
Write the Project Product Description	Once, as part of starting up a project	This is a specialised form of product description, defining the scope, requirements, customer's quality expectations and acceptance criteria
Create the product breakdown structure	For all levels of plan	Break the plan down into the major products to be delivered Further break these down until an appropriate level of detail for the plan is reached
Write Product Descriptions	For all levels of plan	Define the purpose and appearance of the product, its users, level of quality required, creation and checking skills
Draw the product flow diagram	For all levels of plan	Defines the sequence in which the products will be developed and any dependencies between them

3: Techniques

Quality review

A quality review (planned when creating Stage and Team Plans) is a structured assessment of a document conducted by a group of peers in a planned, documented and organised fashion. Its objectives are to:

- assess the conformity of the document against set criteria
- involve key interested parties in checking the document's quality and thus promoting wider acceptance of the product
- provide confirmation that the product is complete and can be approved
- advise that the product can be baselined for configuration management and change control purposes.

Table 32: Four roles of quality review

ROLE	DESCRIPTION
Chair	• Control of preparation, review and follow-up • Sets agenda • Ensures focus
Presenter	• Represents the resource(s) that created the product • Answers questions
Reviewer	• Reviews product during preparation • Completes question list • Annotates the product with any spelling or grammar errors • Gets answers during review • Chooses which follow-up actions to check
ROLE	DESCRIPTION
Administrator	• Organises location • Sends out invitations • Creates follow-up action list of any changes needed • Directed by chair

Table 33: Three steps of quality review

STEP	ACTIVITY
Preparation	<ul><li>Date, location and duration</li><li>Invitations</li><li>Reviewers create question lists and submit to chair</li><li>Product annotated with any spelling or grammar concerns</li><li>Chair creates agenda from question lists in consultation with presenter</li></ul>
Review	<ul><li>Led by chair</li><li>Presenter answers reviewer questions</li><li>Administrator notes any changes on follow-up action list</li><li>Chair identifies who will action and who will check</li></ul>
Follow-up	<ul><li>Changes made checked by reviewers</li><li>Progress chased by administrator</li><li>Chair confirms result to Project Manager</li></ul>

CHAPTER 4: TAILORING

PRINCE2 can be used on any type or size of project. It is designed to be tailored for each project. Tailoring involves using the correct amount of planning and control, and the appropriate level of the processes and themes for a specific project.

The PRINCE2 principles are universal and will always apply. By comparing each principle to the project, the practitioner will understand how to adapt the theme to the project without losing its value.

Existing terms, procedures and forms

There is no problem in changing PRINCE2 terminology for terms long established in an organisation's projects. There is no problem in replacing suggested PRINCE2 forms with existing equivalents. There is no problem in replacing procedures, such as risk or change, with tried-and-tested procedures already embedded in an organisation's culture.

Business Case

All projects should have justification. Small projects may not need all the elements shown in the PRINCE2 Business Case Product Description, but there should always be reasons and a verifiable set of benefits or savings. If you judge that a Business Case is not needed, do you really have a project or is it just a Work Package?

Organisation

Roles can be shared or combined, but PRINCE2 does not recommend sharing the Executive or Project Manager role.

In a small project, the Project Board may be one person, depending on who is supplying the development resources. The Project Manager may absorb the Team Manager role. Project

4: Tailoring

Support may be done by the Project Manager or part time by a member of the development team. The Project Board may do its own Project Assurance.

In a large project, there may need to be more than one Senior User in order to fully represent the user needs. You may need more than one Senior Supplier in order to get supplier commitments. Do remember that an alternative to having several Senior Suppliers could be to make the company's purchasing manager the Senior Supplier. Be wary of having too many Senior Users. Do not let them overwhelm the Project Board. If there genuinely are lots of them, put them in a user group with one spokesperson on the Project Board.

Remember that roles can be changed for different stages. If you no longer need a particular supplier for the next stage, remove that representative from the Senior Supplier role. Similarly, the skills you need for Project Assurance may well change from stage to stage, so don't be afraid to ring the changes.

Documentation

In a small project, documents can be created that comprise several management products. It is therefore possible to manage a small PRINCE2 project with a smaller set of documentation:

- Project Initiation Documentation, including:
    - Project Brief
    - Business Case
    - Risk Management Strategy
    - Quality Management Strategy
    - Configuration Management Strategy
    - Communication Management Strategy
    - Project Plan, which includes:
        - Project Product Description
        - Product Descriptions
    - Benefits Review Plan
- Highlight Reports, which include:
    - Product Status Account
- The Daily Log, including:

4: Tailoring

- o Issues
- o Risks
- o Lessons
- o Planned and actual quality management activities
- Configuration Item Records
- End Project Report, including:
  - o Lessons report

Plans

In a small project, you may not need teams, so no Team Plans. If you have only one development stage, can the detail necessary for day-to-day control be incorporated into the Project Plan?

Quality

For any project you need to know the quality aim and how you will meet that, so you will need the customer's quality expectations and acceptance criteria. Depending on the size of the project, you can then decide if quality needs can be taken care of by writing good Product Descriptions, or whether you need to examine the Quality Management Strategy for other necessary entries.

Risk

Every project should consider its risks. In a small project you may not need a full-blown Risk Management Strategy, but you must review risks before starting out. If you find that there are several serious risks facing the project, you should create a Risk Register in order to keep track of them.

Change

Even the smallest project should be ready for changes or additions. Just having the discipline to record these in the Issue Register should enable you to keep them under control. You

4: Tailoring

may not need to write that part of a Configuration Management Strategy.

You will need to decide how to identify project products and what form of version control is to be used. Once a product reaches a settled form, you should keep it somewhere 'safe' from uncontrolled change.

Progress

Ask yourself who the stakeholders are, even for small projects. Knowing what information to provide, when and how, should be enough, rather than writing a full Communication Management Strategy.

GLOSSARY OF TERMS

BAU – business as usual

BRP – Benefits Review Plan

CIR – Configuration Item Record

CP – Closing a Project (process)

CQE – Customer's Quality Expectations

CS – Controlling a Stage (process)

DP – Directing a Project (process)

Exec – Executive (chairman of the Project Board)

FOAR – Follow-on Action Recommendations

IP – Initiating a Project (process)

ISO – International Standards Organisation

MoSCoW – Must have, Should have, Could have or Won't have

MP – Managing Product Delivery (process)

O-S – Off-Specification

PBP – Product-based Planning

PID – Project Initiation Documentation

PM – Project Manager

PMT – Project Management Team

PRINCE2 – Projects IN a Controlled Environment

RFC – Request For Change

Risk MS – Risk Management Strategy

SB – Managing a Stage Boundary (process)

Glossary of Terms

SS – Senior Supplier (Project Board role)

SU – Senior User (Project Board role)

WP – Work Package

ITG RESOURCES

IT Governance Ltd sources, creates and delivers products and services to meet the real-world, evolving IT governance needs of today's organisations, directors, managers and practitioners.

The ITG website (*www.itgovernance.co.uk*) is the international one-stop-shop for corporate and IT governance information, advice, guidance, books, tools, training and consultancy.

www.itgovernance.co.uk/project_governance.aspx is the information page on our website for project management resources.

Other Websites

Books and tools published by IT Governance Publishing (ITGP) are available from all business booksellers and are also immediately available from the following websites:

www.itgovernance.eu is our euro-denominated website which ships from Benelux and has a growing range of books in European languages other than English.

www.itgovernanceusa.com is a US$-based website that delivers the full range of IT Governance products to North America, and ships from within the continental US.

www.itgovernanceasia.com provides a selected range of ITGP products specifically for customers in the Indian sub-continent.

www.itgovernance.asia delivers the full range of ITGP publications, serving countries across Asia Pacific. Shipping from Hong Kong, US dollars, Singapore dollars, Hong Kong dollars, New Zealand dollars and Thai baht are all accepted through the website.

Toolkits

ITG's unique range of toolkits includes the IT Governance Framework Toolkit, which contains all the tools and guidance that you will need in order to develop and implement an appropriate IT governance framework for your organisation.

For a free paper on how to use the proprietary Calder-Moir IT Governance Framework, and for a free trial version of the toolkit, see *www.itgovernance.co.uk/calder_moir.aspx*.

ITG Resources

There is also a wide range of toolkits to simplify implementation of management systems, such as an ISO/IEC 27001 ISMS or an ISO/IEC 22301 BCMS, and these can all be viewed and purchased online at *www.itgovernance.co.uk*.

Training Services

IT Governance offers an extensive portfolio of training courses designed to educate information security, IT governance, risk management and compliance professionals. Our classroom and online training programmes will help you develop the skills required to deliver best practice and compliance to your organisation. They will also enhance your career by providing you with industry standard certifications and increased peer recognition. Our range of courses offer a structured learning path from Foundation to Advanced level in the key topics of information security, IT governance, business continuity and service management.

Our *Implementing IT Governance: Foundation and Principles* training course delivers introductory training to raise awareness, build knowledge and develop a complete understanding of IT governance and its implementation. It has been specifically designed to show delegates how to create a single integrated management framework that ensures that IT truly supports and delivers on all organisational strategies and objectives.

Full details of all IT Governance training courses can be found at *www.itgovernance.co.uk/training.aspx*.

Professional Services and Consultancy

Our company is an acknowledged world leader in our field. We can use our multi-sector and multi-standard knowledge and experience to help you accelerate your IT GRC (governance, risk, compliance) projects.

We understand that when you are involved in an IT GRC project, you need to be sure that you are making the right decisions, based on the most up to date and accurate information.

When you choose us you can be 100% confident that you will have the best support in the world.

For more information about IT Governance Consultancy Services see *www.itgovernance.co.uk/consulting.aspx*.

ITG Resources

Publishing Services

IT Governance Publishing (ITGP) is the world's leading IT-GRC publishing imprint that is wholly owned by IT Governance Ltd.

With books and tools covering all IT governance, risk and compliance frameworks, we are the publisher of choice for authors and distributors alike, producing unique and practical publications of the highest quality, in the latest formats available, which readers will find invaluable.

www.itgovernancepublishing.co.uk is the website dedicated to ITGP enabling both current and future authors, distributors, readers and other interested parties, to have easier access to more information. This allows ITGP website visitors to keep up to date with the latest publications and news.

Newsletter

IT governance is one of the hottest topics in business today, not least because it is also the fastest moving.

You can stay up to date with the latest developments across the whole spectrum of IT governance subject matter, including; risk management, information security, ITIL and IT service management, project governance, compliance and so much more, by subscribing to ITG's core publications and topic alert emails.

Simply visit our subscription centre and select your preferences: *www.itgovernance.co.uk/newsletter.aspx*.